Christmas 2006

♡ Dear Noelle,

Happiness is having a

Child . . . of being a mother

Love, ♡
Mom & Dad

A Gift From:

_____

Date:

_____

A Spoonful of Sugar For Mothers

A Spoonful of Sugar For Mothers

ISBN: 1-58173-485-9

Book design by Pat Covert

Printed in China

A Spoonful of Sugar
For Mothers

A child's hand in yours—what tenderness and power it arouses. You are instantly the very touchstone of wisdom and strength.
Marjorie Holmes

Instruction does much, but encouragement does everything.
Johann Wolfgang von Goethe

What do girls do who haven't any mothers to help them through their troubles?
Louisa May Alcott

Sugar for Mothers

Children represent God's most generous gift to us.
James Dobson

The greatest lessons I have ever learned were at my mother's knees. … All that I am, or hope to be, I owe to my angel mother.
Abraham Lincoln

A man travels the world over in search of what he needs and returns home to find it.
George Moore

All of us are born for a reason, but all of us don't discover why. Success in life has nothing to do with what you gain in life or accomplish for yourself. It's what you do for others.
Danny Thomas

Having a baby is definitely a labor of love.
Joan Rivers

You leave home to seek your fortune, and when you get it, you go home and share it with your family.
Anita Baker

Sugar for Mothers

A suburban mother's role is to deliver children obstetrically once, and by car forever after.
Peter De Vries

The tie which links mother and child is of such pure and immaculate strength as to be never violated.
Washington Irving

True beauty emanates from a selfless heart.
Cristina Munoz

A light heart lives long.
William Shakespeare

Don't wait for people to be kind;
show them how.
Unknown

A mother is a person who, seeing there are only
four pieces of pie for five people, promptly
announces she never did care for pie.
Tenneva Jordan

Sugar for Mothers

Men are what their mothers made them.
Ralph Waldo Emerson

How beautiful a day can be
when kindness touches it.
George Elliston

If the whole world were put into one scale, and my
mother in the other, the whole world would kick the beam.
Lord Langdale

Some pursue happiness—others create it.
Unknown

Remember not only to say the right thing in the
right place, but far more difficult still, to leave
unsaid the wrong thing at the tempting moment.
Benjamin Franklin

There are times that when truth and kindness
conflict, one ought to choose kindness, especially
when a little honesty is better than a lot.
Leroy Jack Syrop

Sugar for Mothers

For attractive lips, speak words of kindness.
Audrey Hepburn

Our brightest blazes of gladness are commonly
kindled by unexpected sparks.
Samuel Johnson

Tenderness and kindness are not signs of
weakness and despair, but manifestations
of strength and resolution.
Kahlil Gibran

Never doubt that a small group of thoughtful,
committed citizens can change the world.
Indeed, it is the only thing that ever has.
Margaret Mead

When one door of happiness closes, another opens.
Helen Keller

People will forget what you said, people will forget
what you did, but people will never forget
how you made them feel.
Bonnie Jean Wasmund

Joy comes from using your potential.
Will Schultz

Mother's words of wisdom: "Answer me!
Don't talk with food in your mouth!"
Erma Bombeck

As much as we need a prosperous economy, we also
need prosperity of kindness and decency.
Caroline Kennedy Schlossberg

The soul is healed by being with children.
Fyodor Dostoevsky

Happiness is a perfume which you cannot pour on
someone without getting some on yourself.
Ralph Waldo Emerson

Giving is the secret of a healthy life. Not
necessarily money, but whatever a person has
of encouragement, sympathy, and understanding.
John D. Rockefeller, Jr.

You see much more of your children
once they leave home.
Lucille Ball

To change and to change for the better
are two different things.
German Proverb

Love is the master key which opens
the gates of happiness.
Oliver Wendell Holmes

Career mothers are not kidding anybody. Being a mom is the hardest job of all. You got to work to rest.
Sandy Duncan

Happiness is a butterfly, which, when pursued, is always just beyond your grasp, but which, if you will sit down quietly, may alight upon you.
Nathaniel Hawthorne

A hundred men may make an encampment, but it takes a woman to make a home.
Chinese Proverb

Sugar for Mothers

Who in their infinite wisdom decreed that Little League
uniforms be white? Certainly not a mother.
Erma Bombeck

Bear in mind that the wonderful things you learn
in your schools are the work of many generations.
All this is put in your hands as your inheritance
in order that you may receive it, honor it, add to it,
and one day faithfully hand it on to your children.
Albert Einstein

Happiness is having a large, loving, caring,
close-knit family in another city.
George Burns

True happiness is not attained through self-gratification,
but through fidelity to a worthy purpose.
Helen Keller

What are Raphael's Madonnas but the shadow of a
mother's love, fixed in permanent outline forever?
Thomas Wentworth Higginson

Your children tell you casually years later what it would
have killed you with worry to know at the time.
Mignon McLaughlin

16

The thing that impresses me most about America
is the way parents obey their children.
Edward, Duke of Windsor

No matter what you've done for yourself or for
humanity, if you can't look back on having given
love and attention to your own family, what
have you really accomplished?
Lee Iacocca

The strength of a nation derives from
the integrity of the home.
Confucius

A Spoonful of

The love we give away is the only love we keep.
Elbert Hubbard

Children have more need of models than of critics.
Joseph Joubert

Happiness cannot be traveled to, owned, earned, worn
or consumed. Happiness is the spiritual experience of
living every minute with love, grace and gratitude.
Denis Waitley

The most important trip you may take in
life is meeting people half way.
Henry Boyle

Happiness is not an accident. Nor is it something you
wish for. Happiness is something you design.
Jim Rohn

You will never find time for anything.
If you want time, you must make it.
Charles Bixton

The supreme happiness in life is the
conviction that we are loved.
Victor Hugo

Some are kissing mothers and some are
scolding mothers, but it is love just the same,
and most mothers kiss and scold together.
Pearl S. Buck

Insults should be written in the sand,
and praises carved in stone.
Arabic Proverb

You don't really understand human nature unless
you know why a child on a merry-go-round will
wave at his parents every time around—and
why his parents will always wave back.
William D. Tammeus

Smile at each other, smile at your wife, smile at
your husband, smile at your children, smile at each
other—it doesn't matter who it is—and that will help
you to grow up in greater love for each other.
Mother Teresa

Happiness is in the heart, not in the circumstances.
Unknown

You're a happy fellow, for you'll give happiness
and joy to many other people. There is
nothing better or greater than that.
Ludwig van Beethoven

Love is the great miracle cure. Loving
ourselves works miracles in our lives.
Louise Hay

Did you ever see an unhappy horse? Did you ever
see a bird that had the blues? One reason why birds
and horses are not unhappy is because they are
not trying to impress other birds and horses.
Dale Carnegie

Sometimes you make the right decision;
sometimes you make the decision right.
Dr. Phil McGraw

Money will buy you a bed, but not a good night's sleep;
a house but not a home; a companion but not a friend.
Zig Ziglar

Cherishing children is the mark of a civilized society.
Joan Ganz Cooney

Fun is about as good a habit as there is.
Jimmy Buffett

The phrase "working mother" is redundant.
Jane Sellman

A woman invited some people to dinner. At the table,
she turned to her six-year-old daughter and said,
"Would you like to say the blessing?"
"I wouldn't know what to say," the little girl replied.
"Just say what you hear Mommy say, " the mother said.
The little girl bowed her head and said, "Dear Lord, why
on earth did I invite all these people to dinner?"
Unknown

You may have tangible wealth untold;
Caskets of jewels and coffers of gold.
Richer than I you can never be—
I had a mother who read to me.
Strickland Gillilan

I live by this credo: Have a little laugh at life and look
around you for happiness instead of sadness. Laughter
has always brought me out of unhappy situations.
Even in your darkest moment, you usually can find
something to laugh about if you try hard enough.
Red Skelton

What children hear at home soon flies abroad.
Thomas Fuller

To describe my mother would be to write
about a hurricane in its perfect power.
Maya Angelou

The hand that rocks the cradle is
the hand that rules the world.
W. S. Ross

Pleasure is the only thing to live for.
Nothing ages like happiness.
Oscar Wilde

The decision to have a child is to accept that your heart
will forever walk about outside of your body.
Katherine Hadley

The mother-child relationship is very paradoxical. It
requires the most intense love on the mother's side, yet
this very love must help the child grow away from the
mother and become fully independent.
Erich Fromm

Happiness is that state of consciousness which
proceeds from the achievement of one's values.
Ayn Rand

A Spoonful of

I always wanted children, but not until they were
actually part of my life did I realize that I could
love that fiercely, or get that angry.
Cokie Roberts

Anyone who has brought up children knows that
consistency has absolutely nothing to do with discipline.
Bill Cosby

To have joy one must share it.
Happiness was born a twin.
Lord Byron

Sugar for Mothers

As a mother, my job is to take care of what is possible and trust God with the impossible.
Ruth Bell Graham

Motherhood is not for the fainthearted. Frogs, skinned knees, and the insults of teenage girls are not meant for the wimpy.
Danielle Steele

Adults are obsolete children.
Dr. Seuss

Mother's love grows by giving.
Charles Lamb

There is only one happiness in life:
to love and be loved.
George Sand

In the final analysis, it is not what you do
for your children but what you have taught
them to do for themselves that will make
them successful human beings.
Ann Landers

Sugar for Mothers

A man is happy so long as he chooses to be happy.
Alexander Solzhenitsyn

To live happily is an inward power of the soul.
Marcus Aurelius

The adult with a capacity for true maturity is
one who has grown out of childhood
without losing childhood's best traits.
Joseph Stone

Man is most nearly himself when he achieves the seriousness of a child at play.
Heraclitus

The question for the child is not "Do I want to be good?" but "Whom do I want to be like?"
Bruno Bettelheim

Mother love is the fuel that enables a normal human being to do the impossible.
Marion C. Garretty

Sugar for Mothers

Even when freshly-washed and relieved of all
obvious confections, children tend to be sticky.
Fran Lebowitz

There is something in the pang of change
more than the heart can bear, unhappiness
remembering happiness.
Euripides

A child enters your home, and for the next twenty
years makes so much noise you can hardly stand it.
The child departs, leaving the house so silent
you think you are going mad.
John Andrew Holmes

Children possess a remarkable amount of
passion. They throw themselves completely,
heart and soul, into everything.
Mary Lou Retton

Happiness is the meaning and the purpose of life,
the whole aim and end of human existence.
Aristotle

Youth is happy because it has the ability to see
beauty. Anyone who keeps the ability to
see beauty never grows old.
Franz Kafka

Sugar for Mothers

Heaven will be no heaven to me if
I do not meet my wife there.
Andrew Jackson

You can learn many things from children.
How much patience you have, for instance.
Franklin P. Jones

At the end of your life, you will never regret not having
passed one more test, not winning one more verdict, or
not closing one more deal. You will regret time not
spent with a husband, a friend, a child, or a parent.
Barbara Bush

Those who wish to sing always find a song.
Swedish Proverb

Children are likely to live up to
what you believe in them.
Lady Bird Johnson

Happiness is an endowment and not an acquisition.
It depends more upon temperament
and disposition than environment.
John J. Ingalls

Loving a child doesn't mean giving in to all his whims; to love him is to bring out the best in him, to teach him to love what is difficult.
Nadia Boulanger

A man loves his sweetheart the most, his wife the best, but his mother the longest.
Irish Proverb

If we are meant to "love thy neighbor as thyself," then surely we should love the world's children as our own.
Audrey Hepburn

The trouble with being a parent is that by the time
you are experienced, you are unemployed.
Unknown

When you have children yourself, you begin to
understand what you owe your parents.
Japanese Proverb

Never fear spoiling children by making them
happy. Happiness is the atmosphere in
which all good affections grow.
Ann Eliza Bray

Sugar for Mothers

Man needs, for his happiness, not only the enjoyment of this or that, but hope and enterprise and change.
Bertrand Russell

We should learn from children not to hold grudges. Children often fight when they play together, but they quickly make up, and their fights don't deteriorate into bitter feuds.
Joseph Wechsberg

All that I am, my mother made me.
John Quincy Adams

Think of all the beauty still left
around you and be happy.
Anne Frank

The foolish man seeks happiness in the
distance; the wise grows it under his feet.
James Oppenheim

When I grow up, I want to be a little boy.
Joseph Heller

The world is not always a kind place. That's
something all children learn for themselves, whether
we want them to or not, but it's something
they really need our help to understand.
Fred Rogers

A day without laughter is a day wasted.
Charlie Chaplin

Happiness is an expression of the
soul in considered actions.
Aristotle

[A] mother is one to whom you
hurry when you are troubled.
Emily Dickinson

Kids are life's only guaranteed,
bona fide upside surprise.
Jack Nicholson

Level with your child by being honest. Nobody
spots a phony quicker than a child.
Mary MacCracken

Sugar for Mothers

The beauty of "spacing" children many years apart
lies in the fact that parents have time to learn
the mistakes that were made with the older ones—
which permits them to make exactly the opposite
mistakes with the younger ones.
Sydney J. Harris

People are just as happy as they
make up their minds to be.
Abraham Lincoln

A baby is God's opinion that life should go on.
Carl Sandburg

Discipline is a symbol of caring to a child. He needs guidance. If there is love, there is no such thing as being too tough with a child.
Bette Davis

Tell your child often "I love you, no matter what."
Cindy Francis

Only love can be divided endlessly and still not diminish.
Anne Morrow Lindbergh

To this day George Sr. is the soft touch, and I'm the enforcer. I'm the one who writes them a letter and says, "Shape up!" He writes, "You're marvelous."
Barbara Bush

Dreams are what get you started. Discipline is what keeps you going.
Jim Ryun

People take different roads seeking fulfillment and happiness. Just because they're not on your road doesn't mean they've gotten lost.
H. Jackson Brown, Jr.

People think I am disciplined. It is not discipline. It is devotion. There is a great difference.
Luciano Pavarotti

Always end the name of your child with a vowel, so that when you yell, the name will carry.
Bill Cosby

Blessed is the person who can laugh at himself—he'll never cease to be amused.
Unknown

Sugar for Mothers

The moment a child is born, the mother is also born.
She never existed before. The woman existed, but the
mother, never. A mother is something absolutely new.
Rajneesh

In my parents I saw a model where they were
really always communicating, doing things together.
They were really kind of a team. I wanted
some of that magic myself.
Bill Gates

Don't worry that children never listen to you;
worry that they are always watching you.
Robert Fulghum

Parents often talk about the younger generation
as if they didn't have anything to do with it.
Haim Ginott

The main source of good discipline is growing up in a
loving family, being loved, and learning to love in return.
Benjamin Spock

The highest happiness of man ... is to have
probed what is knowable and quietly to
revere what is unknowable.
Johann Wolfgang von Goethe

If you want others to be happy, practice compassion.
If you want to be happy, practice compassion.
Dalai Lama

Some people regard discipline as a chore. For me,
it is a kind of order that sets me free to fly.
Julie Andrews

All mothers are rich when they love their children.
Their love is always the most beautiful of joys.
Maurice Maeterlinck

And forget not that the earth delights to feel your bare
feet and the winds long to play with your hair.
Kahlil Gibran

My mom used to say it doesn't matter how many
kids you have ... because one kid'll take up 100%
of your time, so more kids can't possibly take
up more than 100% of your time.
Karen Brown

Children aren't happy with nothing to ignore,
And that's what parents were created for.
Ogden Nash

Sugar for Mothers

Everyone who deals with teens seems to agree that the most important and toughest job is staying in connection and conversation ... not delivering a lecture but saying what we think.
Ellen Goodman

A child needs your love most
when he deserves it least.
Erma Bombeck

You have to stand for what you believe in. And sometimes you have to stand alone.
Queen Latifah

He is happiest, be he king or peasant,
who finds peace in his home.
Johann Wolfgang von Goethe

Thank God I had two parents who loved
me enough to stay on my case.
Shaquille O'Neal

Because I feel that in the heavens above
The angels, whispering one to another,
Can find among their burning tears of love,
None so devotional as that of "Mother."
Edgar Allan Poe

Sugar for Mothers

You have a wonderful child. Then, when he's thirteen, gremlins carry him away and leave in his place a stranger who gives you not a moment's peace.
Jill Eichenberry

Oh, to be only half as wonderful as my child thought I was when he was small, and only half as stupid as my teenager now thinks I am.
Rebecca Richards

The best substitute for experience is sixteen.
Raymond Duncan

Laughter is the hand of God on the
shoulder of a troubled world.
Zig Ziglar

Through humor, you can soften some of the
worst blows that life delivers. And once you find
laughter, no matter how painful your situation
might be, you can survive it.
Bill Cosby

Some of us might find happiness if we quit
struggling so desperately for it.
William Feather

Sugar for Mothers

Father asked us what was God's noblest work.
Anna said "Men," but I said "Babies." Men
are often bad, but babies never are.
Louisa May Alcott

The best way to cheer yourself up is to
try to cheer somebody else up.
Mark Twain

Chaos in the midst of chaos isn't funny,
but chaos in the midst of order is.
Steve Martin

I know how to do anything—I'm a mom.
Roseanne Barr

To show a child what once delighted you, to find the child's delight added to your own, this is happiness.
J. B. Priestley

If my father was the head of our house,
my mother was its heart.
Irving Pichel

Sugar for Mothers

A mother's arms are made of tenderness,
and children sleep soundly in them.
Victor Hugo

The child supplies the power, but the
parents have to do the steering.
Benjamin Spock

A mother is the truest friend we have.
Washington Irving

Govern a family as you would cook
a small fish—very gently.
Chinese Proverb

Success is getting what you want;
happiness is wanting what you get.
Dale Carnegie

My mother protected me from the world,
and my father threatened me with it.
Quentin Crisp

What you teach your own children is
what you really believe in.
Cathy Warner Weatherford

Friendships come and go,
but families are forever.
Kenny Rogers

You know the only people who are always
sure about the proper way to raise children?
Those who've never had any.
Bill Cosby

What makes people happy is activity; changing evil itself into good by power, working in a God-like manner.
Johann Wolfgang von Goethe

Call it a clan, call it a network, call it a tribe, call it a family. Whatever you call it, whoever you are, you need one.
Jane Howard

The first half of our lives is ruined by our parents, and the second half by our children.
Clarence Darrow

Some cause happiness wherever they go;
others whenever they go.
Oscar Wilde

It's funny what happens when you become
a grandparent. You start to act all goofy and do
things you never thought you'd do. It's terrific.
Mike Krzyzewski

Home is where one starts from.
T. S. Eliot

Home is the place where, when you have to go there, they have to take you in.
Robert Frost

Meditate. Live purely. Be quiet. Do your work with mastery. Like the moon, come out from behind the clouds! Shine.
Buddha

In every conceivable manner, the family is a link to our past, a bridge to our future.
Alex Haley

Life began with waking up and
loving my mother's face.
George Eliot

The best chance for success in raising children is if
the parents themselves set the right standards by
their own example. Children need to see that the results
of those standards imposed on them are beneficial.
Daya Mata

Happiness is not a reward—it is a consequence.
Suffering is not a punishment—it is a result.
Robert Green Ingersoll

A child is a person who can't understand why
someone would give away a perfectly good kitten.
Doug Larson

To put the world right in order, we must first
put the nation in order; to put the nation in order,
we must first put the family in order; to put the
family in order, we must first cultivate our
personal life; we must first set our hearts right.
Confucius

Dedicate yourself to the good you deserve and desire
for yourself. Give yourself peace of mind. You
deserve to be happy. You deserve delight.
Mark Victor Hansen

Sugar for Mothers

You are the master of your emotions. Choosing
to be happy or unhappy depends entirely on
you. So why not choose to be happy?

M. K. Soni

When God thought of mother, He must have laughed
with satisfaction, and framed it quickly—
so rich, so deep, so divine, so full of soul,
power, and beauty, was the conception.

Henry Ward Beecher

One lamp—thy mother's love—amid the stars
Shall lift its pure flame changeless, and before
The throne of God, burn through eternity—
Holy—as it was lit and lent thee here.

Nathaniel Parker Willis

Perhaps the greatest social service that can
be rendered by anybody to this country
and to mankind is to bring up a family.
George Bernard Shaw

That best academy, a mother's knee.
James Russell Lowell

To an adolescent, there is nothing in the world
more embarrassing than a parent.
Dave Barry

The voice of parents is the voice of gods, for to their children they are heaven's lieutenants.
William Shakespeare

Sweater, n.: garment worn by child when its mother is feeling chilly.
Ambrose Bierce

Nothing can bring a real sense of security into the home except true love.
Billy Graham

Being a full-time mother is one of the highest salaried jobs... since the payment is pure love.
Mildred B. Vermont

There are two lasting bequests we can give our children. One is roots. The other is wings.
Hodding Carter, Jr.

Blaming mother is just a negative way of clinging to her still.
Nancy Friday

A smile is a curved line that sets things straight.
Unknown

In the path of our happiness shall we find the learning
for which we have chosen this lifetime.
Richard Bach

It kills you to see them grow up. But I guess
it would kill you quicker if they didn't.
Barbara Kingsolver

I'm fulfilled in what I do. I never thought that a lot of money or fine clothes—the finer things of life—would make you happy. My concept of happiness is to be filled in a spiritual sense.
Coretta Scott King

Have you any idea how many kids it takes to turn off one light in the kitchen? Three. It takes one to say, "What light?" and two more to say, "I didn't turn it on."
Erma Bombeck

You are forgiven for your happiness and your successes only if you generously consent to share them.
Albert Camus

Sugar for Mothers

A five-year-old said grace at family dinner one night. "Dear God, thank you for these pancakes." When he concluded, his parents asked him why he thanked God for pancakes when they were having chicken. He smiled and said, "I thought I'd see if He was paying attention tonight."
Unknown

Children are not casual guests in our home. They have been loaned to us temporarily for the purpose of loving them and instilling a foundation of values on which their future lives will be built.
James Dobson

Life is hard. After all, it kills you.
Katharine Hepburn

Different men seek after happiness in different ways and by different means, and so make for themselves different modes of life and forms of government.
Aristotle

The family is where most of our joy comes from.
Aidan Quinn

If you want children to keep their feet on the ground, put some responsibility on their shoulders.
Abigail Van Buren

I have been asked hundreds of times in my life why God allows tragedy and suffering. I have to confess that I really do not know the answer totally, even to my own satisfaction. I have to accept, by faith, that God is sovereign, and He is a God of love and mercy and compassion in the midst of suffering.

Billy Graham

Even if happiness forgets you a little bit, never completely forget about it.

Jacques Prévert

Housework, if you do it right, will kill you.

Erma Bombeck

Seek not happiness too greedily,
and be not fearful of unhappiness.
Lao Tzu

A mother's happiness is like a beacon, lighting
up the future but reflected also on the past
in the guise of fond memories.
Honoré de Balzac

A little boy's prayer: "Dear God, please take care of
my daddy and my mommy and my sister and my
brother and my doggy and me. Oh, please take
care of yourself, God. If anything happens to
you, we're gonna be in a big mess."
Unknown

Sugar for Mothers

You have to love your children unselfishly.
That's hard. But it's the only way.
Barbara Bush

Happiness lies in the joy of achievement
and the thrill of creative effort.
Franklin D. Roosevelt

Children who are read to learn two things:
First, that reading is worthwhile, and
second, that they are worthwhile.
Laura Bush

I cannot forget my mother. She is my bridge.
When I needed to get across, she steadied
herself long enough for me to run across safely.
Renita Weems

If you can't make it better, you can laugh at it.
Erma Bombeck

One Sunday in a Midwest city a young child was "acting
up" during the morning worship hour. The parents did
their best to maintain some sense of order but were
losing the battle. Finally the father picked the little fellow
up and walked sternly up the aisle on his way out. Just
before reaching the safety of the foyer, the little one called
loudly to the congregation, "Pray for me! Pray for me!"
Unknown

Perfect love sometimes does not
come until the first grandchild.
Welsh Proverb

Listen to your mother. Mothers are always right.
Brian Baldinger

Don't throw away your friendship with your
teenager over behavior that has no great moral
significance. There will be plenty of real issues
that require you to stand like a rock. Save your
big guns for those crucial confrontations.
James Dobson

Action may not always bring happiness, but there is no happiness without action.
Benjamin Disraeli

No amount of law enforcement can solve a problem that goes back to the family.
J. Edgar Hoover

Most of all the other beautiful things in life come by twos and threes, by dozens and hundreds. Plenty of roses, stars, sunsets, rainbows, brothers and sisters, aunts and cousins, comrades and friends—but only one mother in the whole world.
Kate Douglas Wiggin

Sugar for Mothers

If you want to be happy for a year, plant a garden; if you want to be happy for life, plant a tree.
English Proverb

Mother: the most beautiful word on the lips of mankind.
Kahlil Gibran

Of all the rights of women, the greatest is to be a mother.
Lin Yutang

Happiness is a by-product of an effort to
make someone else happy.
Gretta Brooker Palmer

If you bungle raising your children, I don't think
whatever else you do matters very much.
Jacqueline Kennedy Onassis

The good life, as I conceive it, is a happy life. I do
not mean that if you are good you will be happy;
I mean that if you are happy, you will be good.
Bertrand Russell

Sugar for Mothers

I love acting, but it's much more fun
taking the kids to the zoo.
Nicole Kidman

Happiness or unhappiness is
often a matter of choice.
Unknown

Children in a family are like flowers in a bouquet:
There's always one determined to face in an opposite
direction from the way the arranger desires.
Marcelene Cox

Biology is the least of what makes
someone a mother.
Oprah Winfrey

The heart of a mother is a deep abyss at the bottom of
which you will always find forgiveness.
Honoré de Balzac

And this particular four-year-old prayed: "And
forgive us our trash baskets as we forgive
those who put trash in our baskets."
Unknown

Sugar for Mothers

As long as you can still be disappointed,
you are still young.
Sarah Churchill

Grown don't mean nothing to a mother. A child is a
child. They get bigger, older, but grown? What's that
suppose to mean? In my heart it don't mean a thing.
Toni Morrison

Three grand essentials to happiness in this life
are something to do, something to love,
and something to hope for.
Joseph Addison

There are only two things a child will share willingly:
communicable diseases and his mother's age.
Benjamin Spock

If a child annoys you, quiet him by brushing his hair.
If this doesn't work, use the other side of the
brush on the other end of the child.
Unknown

A wasted youth is better by far than a
wise and productive old age.
Mary Alice Messenger

It is at our mother's knee that we acquire our noblest and truest and highest ideals.
Mark Twain

The childless experts on child-raising also bring tears of laughter to my eyes when they say, "I love children because they're so honest." There is not an agent in the CIA or the KGB who knows how to conceal the theft of food, how to fake being asleep, or how to forge a parent's signature like a child.
Bill Cosby

Children are poor men's riches.
English Proverb

To bring up a child in the way he should go,
travel that way yourself once in a while.
Josh Billings

Your children need your presence
more than your presents.
Jesse Jackson

There are as many nights as days, and the one is
just as long as the other in the year's course.
Even a happy life cannot be without a measure
of darkness, and the word "happy" would lose
its meaning if it were not balanced by sadness.
Carl Jung

Knowledge of what is possible is
the beginning of happiness.
George Santayana

Children begin by loving their parents. After a time they
judge them. Rarely, if ever, do they forgive them.
Oscar Wilde

Boys will be boys. And even that wouldn't matter if
only we could prevent girls from being girls.
Anthony Hope Hawkins

An aware parent loves all children he or she meets
and interacts with—for you are a caretaker for
those moments in time.
Doc Childre

Laughter is the shortest distance
between two people.
Victor Borge

The quickest way for a parent to get a child's
attention is to sit down and look comfortable.
Lane Olinghouse

Sugar for Mothers

There are three ways to get something done:
do it yourself, employ someone, or
forbid your children to do it.
Monta Crane

I love to play hide-and-seek with my kid, but some
days my goal is to find a hiding place where he
can't find me until after high school.
Unknown

The age of your children is a key factor in how quickly
you are served in a restaurant. We once had a waiter in
Canada who said, "Could I get you your check?" and
we answered, "How about the menu first?"
Erma Bombeck

A mother's love for her child is like nothing else in the world. It knows no law, no pity, it dares all things and crushes down remorselessly all that stands in its path.
Agatha Christie

One good mother is worth a hundred schoolmasters.
George Herbert

Mother's love is peace. It need not be acquired; it need not be deserved.
Erich Fromm

Sugar for Mothers

Who ran to help me when I fell,
And would some pretty story tell,
Or kiss the place to make it well?
My mother.
Ann Taylor

Parents are often so busy with the physical rearing of
children that they miss the glory of parenthood, just as
the grandeur of the trees is lost when raking leaves.
Marcelene Cox

The truth is that parents are not really interested
in justice. They just want quiet.
Bill Cosby

No one in the world can take
the place of your mother.
Harry Truman

The best way to make children good
is to make them happy.
Oscar Wilde

If you want to recapture your youth,
just cut off his allowance.
Red Buttons

There is only one way to happiness, and that is to cease worrying about the things which are beyond the power of our will.
Epictetus

There's no such thing as fun for the whole family.
Jerry Seinfeld

Never raise your hand to your children; it leaves your midsection unprotected.
Miriam Robbins

The trouble with children is
that they are not returnable.
Fyodor Dostoyevski

Children are a great comfort in your old age—
and they help you reach it faster, too.
Lionel Kauffman

It's frightening to think that you mark your
children merely by being yourself. It seems
unfair. You can't assume the responsibility
for everything you do—or don't do.
Simone De Beauvoir

Sugar for Mothers

A mother is not a person to lean on, but
a person to make leaning unnecessary.
Dorothy Canfield Fisher

Let the child's first lesson be obedience,
and the second will be what thou wilt.
Benjamin Franklin

By the time a man realizes that maybe his father was
right, he usually has a son who thinks he's wrong.
Charles Wadsworth

I can't tell my children to reach for the sun.
All I can do is reach for it myself.
Joyce Maynard

No matter how calmly you try to referee, parenting will
eventually produce bizarre behavior, and I'm not talking
about the kids. Their behavior is always normal.
Bill Cosby

Before I got married, I had six theories about bringing
up children; now I have six children, and no theories.
John Wilmot

A little girl, asked where her home
was, replied, "Where mother is."
Keith L. Brooks

Never lend your car to anyone to
whom you have given birth.
Erma Bombeck

I slept and dreamt that life was joy. I awoke
and saw that life was service. I acted
and behold, service was joy.
Rabindranath Tagore

If high heels were so wonderful, men
would still be wearing 'em.
Sue Grafton

I'm not going to vacuum 'til Sears
makes one you can ride on.
Roseanne Barr

In spite of the six thousand manuals on child-raising in
the bookstores, child-raising is still a dark continent,
and no one really knows anything. You just need a lot
of love and luck—and, of course, courage.
Bill Cosby

Sugar for Mothers

Mother—that was the bank where we
deposited all our hurts and worries.
T. DeWitt Talmage

The more you praise and celebrate your life,
the more there is in life to celebrate.
Oprah Winfrey

Remember, happiness doesn't depend
upon who you are or what you have; it
depends solely upon what you think.
Dale Carnegie

Never have more children than
you have car windows.
Erma Bombeck

I want to have children, but my friends scare me.
One of my friends told me she was in labor for
36 hours. I don't even want to do anything
that feels good for 36 hours.
Rita Rudner

The strength of women comes from the fact
that psychology cannot explain us. Men
can be analyzed, women merely adored.
Oscar Wilde

Sugar for Mothers

The power I exert on the court depends on the
power of my arguments, not on my gender.
Sandra Day O'Connor

Your success as a family, our success as a
society, depends not on what happens in the White
House, but on what happens inside your house.
Barbara Bush

There is only one pretty child in the
world, and every mother has it.
Chinese Proverb

If evolution really works, how come
mothers only have two hands?
Milton Berle

It is sometimes easier to head an institute for
the study of child guidance than it is to turn
one brat into a decent human being.
Joseph Wood Krutch

She never quite leaves her children at home, even
when she doesn't take them along.
Margaret Culkin Banning

Sugar for Mothers

The mere sense of living is joy enough.
Emily Dickinson

A mother was listening to her child say his prayer "Dear Harold." At this, mom interrupted and said, "Wait a minute. How come you called God Harold?" The little boy looked up and said, "That's what they call Him in church. You know the prayer we say, 'Our Father, who art in Heaven, Harold be Thy name.'"
Unknown

Human beings are the only creatures on earth that allow their children to come back home.
Bill Cosby

Happiness is a state of activity.
Aristotle

No one has a right to consume
happiness without producing it.
Helen Keller

Joy is not in things; it is in us.
Richard Wagner

Sugar for Mothers

Use your health, even to the point of wearing it
out. That is what it is for. Spend all you have
before you die; do not outlive yourself.
Bernard Shaw

No painter's brush, nor poet's pen
In justice to her fame
Has ever reached half high enough
To write a mother's name.
Unknown

We do not sing because we are happy;
we are happy because we sing.
William James

The perfection of wisdom and the end of true
philosphy is to proportion our wants to our
possessions, our ambitions to our capacities;
we will then be a happy and a virtuous people.
Mark Twain

Nothing I've ever done has given me more joys and
rewards than being a father to my children.
Bill Cosby

One thing they never tell you about child-raising
is that for the rest of your life, at the drop of a hat,
you are expected to know your child's
name and how old he or she is.
Erma Bombeck

Sugar for Mothers

One ought every day at least to hear a little song, read a good poem, see a fine picture, and, if it were possible, to speak a few reasonable words.
Johann Wolfgang von Goethe

I've learned from experience that the greater part of our happiness or misery depends on our dispositions and not on our circumstances.
Martha Washington

Necessity of action takes away the fear of the act, and makes bold resolution the favorite of fortune.
Francis Quarles

Family has always been the most important
thing in my life. The only real goal that I
ever had was to be a good mother.
Goldie Hawn

Life is too beautiful to be so unhappy about temporary
things. Solve them if you may—or forget them.
Jolynn Teoh Chooi Ling

You can't have a better tomorrow if you
are thinking about yesterday all the time.
Charles F. Kettering

Silence may be golden, but can you think of a better way to entertain someone than to listen to him?
Brigham Young

Don't find fault; find a remedy.
Henry Ford

Youth fades; love droops; the leaves of friendship fall; a mother's secret hope outlives them all.
Oliver Wendell Holmes

Having a child is surely the most beautifully irrational
act that two people in love can commit.
Bill Cosby

A happy family is but an earlier heaven.
John Bowring

The hardest part of raising a child is teaching them to
ride bicycles. A shaky child on a bicycle for the first
time needs both support and freedom. The realization
that this is what the child will always need can hit hard.
Sloan Wilson

Nothing preaches better than the act.
Benjamin Franklin

It's easier to go down a hill than up it, but
the view is much better at the top.
Arnold Bennet

An exasperated mother, whose son was always getting
into mischief, finally asked him, "How do you expect to
get into Heaven?" The boy thought it over and said,
"Well, I'll run in and out and in and out and keep
slamming the door until St. Peter says, 'For Heaven's
sake, Dylan, come in or stay out!'"
Unknown

Humans are the only animals that have
children on purpose with the exception
of guppies, who like to eat theirs.
P.J. O'Rourke

Laughter is the sun that drives
winter from the human face.
Victor Hugo

It would seem that something which means
poverty, disorder, and violence every single day
should be avoided entirely, but the desire
to beget children is a natural urge.
Phyllis Diller

Sugar for Mothers

Happiness is not something you postpone for the future; it is something you design for the present.
Jim Rohn

Sometimes if you want to see a change for the better, you have to take things into your own hands.
Clint Eastwood

Mother Nature, in her infinite wisdom, has instilled within each of us a powerful biological instinct to reproduce; this is her way of assuring that the human race, come what may, will never have any disposable income.
Dave Barry

Building a better you is the first step
to building a better America.
Zig Ziglar

Troubles are often the tools by which
God fashions us for better things.
Henry Ward Beecher

Why do grandparents and grandchildren get along so
well? They have the same enemy—the mother.
Claudette Colbert

Sugar for Mothers

My kids always perceived the bathroom as
a place where you wait it out until all the
groceries are unloaded from the car.
Erma Bombeck

Parenthood is a lot easier to get into than out of.
Bruce Lansky

Happiness makes up in height for
what it lacks in length.
Robert Frost

Motherhood is priced
Of God, at price no man may dare
To lessen or misunderstand.
Helen Hunt Jackson

The way to happiness: keep your heart free from hate,
your mind from worry. Live simply, expect little, give
much. Fill your life with love. Scatter sunshine.
Norman Vincent Peale

God could not be everywhere, so he created mothers.
Jewish Proverb